Family Vacation

Family Vacation

Susan Sessions Rugh

GIBBS SMITH
TO ENRICH AND INSPIRE HUMANKIND

Salt Lake City | Charleston | Santa Fe | Santa Barbara

First Edition
13 12 11 10 09   5 4 3 2 1

Published by
Gibbs Smith
P.O. Box 667
Layton, Utah 84041

Orders: 1.800.835.4993
www.gibbs-smith.com

Designed by Kurt Wahlner
Printed and bound in China
Gibbs Smith books are printed on either recycled, 100% post-consumer waste, or FSC-certified papers.

Preceding overleaf images from Ford Dealers of New England. National Geographic, 1954.

Library of Congress Cataloging-in-Publication Data

Rugh, Susan Sessions.
  Family vacation / Susan Sessions Rugh. — 1st ed.
    p. cm.
  ISBN-13: 978-1-4236-0118-0
  ISBN-10: 1-4236-0118-1
  1. Family vacations—United States—History—20th century. 2. Family vacations—Social aspects—United States. I. Title.
  E161.R86 2008
  973.92—dc22
                            2008040743

Road Map

Acknowledgments

My many thanks to the following people:

Susan Whetstone, Curator of Photography at the Utah Historical Society, who taught me how to select the best photographs and shared snapshots and memories.

Tiffany Taylor, my research assistant, who compiled the photographic database and returned at the last minute to help with finishing touches.

Those who loaned me precious photos of family vacations, especially my students.

My father, whose slide collection was the inspiration for the idea of picturing family vacations.

And finally to Gibbs Smith, who made the book possible, and my editor, Katie Newbold, who has the patience of a saint.

The Rise of the Family Road Trip

The popularity of the family vacation rose after the end of World War II in 1945 when the family vacation became democratized by the road trip. Record numbers of parents loaded the luggage in the trunk of the family car, stashed the children in the back seat, and drove America's highways together. Almost half of all Americans surveyed by the Gallup organization in 1954 said they planned on a summer vacation, most for a week or longer. The 1962 National Recreation Survey stated that during the previous year, Americans "took nearly 80 million vacations on which they spent $6.9 billion, traveled more than 100 billion passenger-miles and remained away from home more than 800 million person-days."

Americans believed in family togetherness and hoped that a vacation together would strengthen family bonds. Unprecedented prosperity and the new two-week paid vacation benefit meant most middle-class families could afford to vacation. In order to travel, Americans rode the wave of postwar consumerism, buying a roomy family car for the vacation or a carload of camping equipment, all necessary items to make a comfortable trip for the whole family. Rising rates of automobile ownership facilitated the family road trip. In 1948, half of all households owned cars, a share that rose to 77 percent in 1960 and 82 percent in 1970. Gas was cheap—only 28 cents a gallon in 1954. American families drove on newly paved roads built by the federal government, ate at roadside restaurants, and stayed the night at modern motels. Families could choose from a variety of vacation destinations: historic sites,

Vacation movies... so gloriously colorful

...so easy to make and afford

That wonderful trip can last for years—for today home movies are so inexpensive they're "part of life" in a million-and-a-half American homes.

Faraway places . . . happy yesterdays . . . spring to joyous life whenever you wish, in movies you make yourself.

Back in the saddle again . . . in your home movies. The precious record brings back *all* the fun of each action-packed day.

"Remember when?" You can't *help* remembering what you saw . . . and did . . . in movies that today are snapshot-simple.

Wild . . . woolly . . . wonderfully colorful. Home movies catch all the warmth and reality . . . the very *color* of life itself.

That grin you know so well . . . the familiar gestures and expressions that *are* your loved ones . . . they're *all* there in movies.

End of the trail—but just the beginning of your enjoyment of that happy day. In movies you live it over and over again.

Vacations . . . celebrations . . . *important* days are safe in movies so easy and inexpensive you should be enjoying them, too.

amusement parks, national parks, or beaches and lakes with their cool water so refreshing in the summer heat.

The family road trip helped Americans understand their status as citizens in the American nation. American parents took their children on pilgrimages to national monuments, from the White House to Old Faithful, to cultivate a sense of civic identity and attachment to American history. In the postwar period, that was true for all, even excluded groups like African Americans who had to fight for their full rights as citizens to travel freely, including the right to public accommodations.

By the 1970s, the golden age of family vacations had come to an end. Three decades of postwar expansion fizzled with the 1973 oil embargo and a recession, squeezing family budgets. The family vacation had lost its cachet. More middle-class Americans could afford to travel to Europe, and a new generation rebelled against the authority of their parents. The end of an era of unparalleled abundance coincided with a shift in cultural authority as baby boomers came of age in a time of sexual revolution, women's liberation, and youth radicalism. The travel industry relinquished the image of the white middle-class suburban family in favor of niche marketing strategies to woo consumers.

Today's aging baby boomers may not have realized it, but the family vacation taught them about their country, how to be citizens, how to explore the unknown. Family travel was for some a life-changing experience that directed them toward a new place to live or toward a life's vocation. Whether you remember the sights you saw or the fights in the back seat, the family vacation is not forgotten. Those memories bring back not only our childhoods but also a time and place in America that no longer exists. But the pictures tell us stories and remind us of the cultural rituals of the vacation—from planning and packing to sightseeing and remembering all the places we have been and the times we shared together as a family.

FACING: Snapshots and home movies helped Americans recall their family vacation memories. Kodak advertisement, 1952.

CHAPTER 1

Planning the Family Vacation

The family vacation required careful planning and budgeting. Oil companies helped their customers get on the road (and consume their products) by publishing travel guides small enough to fit into the car's glove compartment. The guides explained in detail how to budget for a trip, what to pack, how to entertain children, and how to have the car serviced for the trip. From what route to take to what motel to choose, the travel guides prepared family vacationers for the big road trip.

Host of the highways
Refresh at the familiar red cooler on the road to anywhere

The Rand McNally map company also published various types of travel guides, including vacation guides and camping-and-trailer guides. Travel guides combined maps and texts to offer prepackaged travel itineraries that assured travelers a safe and secure journey. Vacationers depended upon commercial atlases and the maps produced for free distribution by gasoline service stations. The covers of maps often depicted families as a way of promoting travel to vacationers. Service stations stopped handing out free maps in the 1970s, so travelers began to rely more on the American Automobile Association and state tourism offices to help them plan their trips.

ABOVE: Companies used road travel to sell their products, as shown in this advertisement for Coca-Cola. *LIFE,* April 1950.

LEFT: The Robert Herrick family of Davenport, Iowa, on vacation in Southern California in 1953. Photographer Rupert Allen. *Look* Magazine Photograph Collection, Library of Congress.

Travel
Colorado
with
CONOCO

Daily Family Vacation Expenses

$2.60   Entertainment and tips
$3.30   Food per person
$4   Lodging per person
$8.40   Gasoline and tolls (300 miles)

Carol Lane, Traveling by Car: A Family Planning Guide to Better Vacations *(1954)*

Checklist for the Trip

Pencils	Towel
Balls	Crackers or fruit
First aid kit	Surprise bag
Vinegar	Camera and film
Tissues	Paper cups
Scissors	Wax bags
Stamps	Blanket, pillow
Lollipops	Thermos of water
Washcloth	Smallest favorite doll

Frances W. Keene, Travel Fun Book for Boys and Girls *(1954)*

Map covers depicted happy families on vacation. Conoco, *Travel Colorado with Conoco*, 1947.

Women's Two – Week Vacation Wardrobe

1 Travel suit (skirt, jacket, blouse) of lightweight wool in neutral tones

1 Evening dress with "prim or plunging" neckline

1 Spectator sports ensemble (wrap-around skirt, halter top, bolero jacket)

1 Rugged life costume (sports blouse and shorts or pedal pushers)

1 Pair of low-heeled shoes

1 Roomy purse

1 Evening clutch and stole

2 Scarves

2 Belts

1 Raincoat and drizzle boots

1 Nightgown and robe

2 Slips

2 Bras

2 Pairs of gloves

3 Pairs of panties

3 Pairs of stockings

1 Bathing suit and beach cover-up

Carol Lane, Traveling by Car: A Family Planning Guide to Better Vacations (1954)

Complete touring information

STATE FARM
ROAD ATLAS

United States ✳ Mexico ✳ Canada ✳ Alaska

Your State Farm Agent is

STATE FARM INSURANCE COMPANIES AUTO LIFE FIRE

Rand McNally's 1960 *State Farm Road Atlas* featured symbols of local culture to represent regional identity. Harold B. Lee Library, Brigham Young University.

What to Pack for the Car

Sandwich supplies

Snacks of fruits, raisins, and canned juices

Empty ice cream carton and rag in case of motion sickness

Toys

Books

Games

Maps

Sunglasses

First aid kit

Sun lotion

Pillows and blankets

Mattress for back seat

Bottle warmer

Carol Lane, Traveling by Car: A Family Planning Guide to Better Vacations *(1954)*

Vacation Lunches

Pineapple juice

Toasted ham sandwiches

Kidney bean salad

Coffee, milk

Assorted fruit

Make at least two sandwiches per person. More if you belong to a very hungry family. Cut bread fairly thin, butter, and spread with mayonnaise. Fill with generous slice of ham, lettuce leaf, and several slices of pickle. Toast lightly, cut diagonally, and wrap each sandwich in oiled paper.

Child Life *(June 1941)*

WESTERN UNITED STATES

------- See America's Scenic Wonders -------

SINCLAIR

Maps promoted national travel in campaigns that capitalized on patriotic themes such as "See the Wonders of America." Sinclair, *Western United States*, circa 1950s.

When starting on a trip—make certain that your car is in good condition before starting on a summer outing. Brakes, steering mechanism, lights, tires and other vital parts should be thoroughly inspected. Remember, too, that the older your car gets, the more carefully it should be checked mechanically.

16

COURTESY OF
SKELLY OIL COMPANY

ABOVE: Highway map of Kansas. Skelly Oil Company, 1960.

LEFT: The Metropolitan Life Insurance Company reminded motorists to service their cars before going on vacation, 1951.

Oil companies coined slogans like "Happy Motoring" to sell their products to families on vacation. Esso, *Washington, D.C. and Vicinity Map and Visitors Guide*, 1957.

ABOVE: States adopted clever slogans to attract "the tourist dollar." *Utah, The Friendly State*, 1947.

RIGHT: Road maps were works of art, beckoning Americans out into the landscape. Chevron Oil Company, *Utah Points of Interest and Touring Map*, 1952.

VOLUME CI NUMBER SIX

The NATIONAL GEOGRAPHIC MAGAZINE

JUNE, 1952

New Map of Southwest Asia
37½ by 27 Inches, in 10 Colors

Sixty-four Pages of Illustrations in Color

PUBLISHED BY THE
NATIONAL GEOGRAPHIC SOCIETY
WASHINGTON, D. C.

$6.00 A YEAR   60c THE COPY

ABOVE: Images of families in maps helped travelers imagine themselves in that landscape. *New York*, Esso, 1956.

LEFT: *National Geographic* featured articles about places to visit in America. *National Geographic*, June 1952.

License Plate Game

"Many license plate numbers spell actual words when decoded with the key on the next page [shown below]. As you pass other cars, write down their license numbers. When you have collected several, start to decode them. You may do it by single numbers or in pairs up to 25. Some license numbers will give you a choice, and by trial and error you may find a word. The winner is the one with the most words at the end of the trip, or set a time limit."

A	B	C	D	E	F	G	H	I	J	K	L	M	N
0	1	2	3	4	5	6	7	8	9	10	11	12	13

O	P	Q	R	S	T	U	V	W	X	Y	Z
14	15	16	17	18	19	20	21	22	23	24	25

Frances W. Keene, Travel Fun Book for Boys and Girls *(1954)*

Calling Slogans

"One player calls a well-known slogan, such as 'The pause that refreshes.' The first player to spy a billboard with that slogan gets a point and may call the next one."

Frances W. Keene, Travel Fun Book for Boys and Girls *(1954)*

Tourettes
by Carol Lane

WOMEN'S TRAVEL DIRECTOR · SHELL OIL COMPANY

Carol Lane, Shell Oil Company's women's travel director, invented the concept of shorter tours, or "tourettes," for family trips. Shell Oil Co., *Tourettes*, 1959.

A children's board game taught geography through imaginary travel. Parker Brothers Inc., "Across the Continent," 1952.

Song: John Brown's Baby

John Brown's baby had a cold upon its chest.
John Brown's baby had a cold upon its chest.
John Brown's baby had a cold upon its chest.
So they rubbed it with camphorated oil.

Sing this verse to the tune of *John Brown's Body*. It is to be sung five times in all, the first time as it reads. For the succeeding verses, certain gestures are substituted for given words, as follows:

1. Substitute motion of rocking folded arms each time the word "baby" occurs.
2. Substitute arm rocking plus pretending to sneeze each time the word "cold" occurs.
3. Substitute arm rocking, sneezing plus thumping the chest each time the word "chest" occurs.
4. Substitute arm rocking, sneezing, thumping plus rubbing the chest for the phrase "rubbed it" in the last line.

Frances W. Keene, **Travel Fun Book for Boys and Girls** *(1954)*

[Author note: My family actually sang this song on the road!]

By providing free road maps, oil companies promoted travel while selling their products. H. M. Gousha Company, circa 1960. Author's collection.

CHAPTER 2 *Hitting the Road*

The family car was like a home on wheels. It buffered the family from the outside world and increased their sense of security while they traveled to unfamiliar places. Car manufacturers emphasized the home-like quality of the car, just like a "living room on wheels." The station wagon was the iconic family car, roomy enough for the bigger postwar family and its gear. Station wagon production peaked in 1956, when 340,000 Ford wagons rolled off the assembly lines, each costing about $2,000. Consumer choices about family cars were shaped by what buyers thought would work for the family vacation. Since going on vacation as a family meant taking the children along, parents were advised to load their suitcases between the front and back seats to create a level surface on which they could place a crib mattress. This "play pen" made a contained space for children where they could rest or play with their toys in the back seat.

In the postwar vacation boom, roadside restaurants like Burger King, McDonald's, and Howard Johnson's began to cater to the family traveler. The atmosphere was wholesome, a blend of soda fountain and dining room. Food service was quick and dependable, and offered menu items children

ABOVE: Oil company maps pictured their dealers as able to meet the needs of families traveling with children. Phillips 66, *Highway Map of Idaho,* 1963.

LEFT: A family picnics along the Natchez Trace Parkway, 1959. Photographer Jack E. Boucher. Courtesy of National Park Service Historic Photograph Collection.

would eat at affordable prices. A burger, fries, and a milk shake replaced the bologna sandwich as family vacation food, making less work for mother.

The family vacation craze also spurred the growth of the motel industry. The word "motel" was coined in San Luis Obispo, California, in 1926, but did not become a standard term for roadside lodging until the 1950s. Motels replaced campgrounds or tourist homes because travelers valued safety, comfort, and convenience, and were willing to pay more for amenities like swimming pools. Families

In 1954, the advertising slogan "There's always room for one more in a Ford Ranch Wagon!" sold American consumers on the idea of a roomy car for "young and rambling" families.

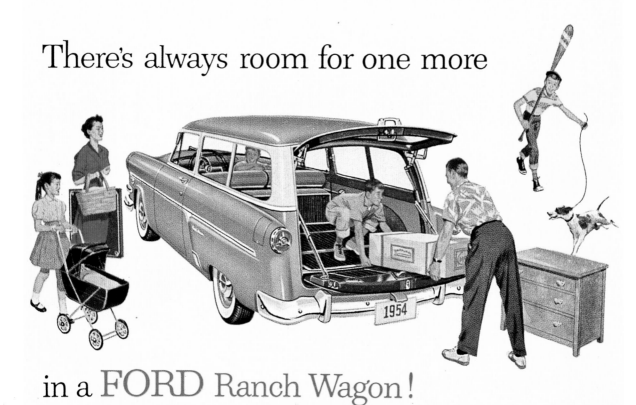

There's always room for one more

in a FORD Ranch Wagon!

seeking reliable lodging enthusiastically welcomed the development of franchise motor hotels in the late 1950s. Kemmons Wilson invented the nationwide branded motel franchise, Holiday Inn, in 1953, after being charged extra for his children at motels on a family trip. After building the first 120-room Holiday Inn in Memphis, he sold blueprints to builders, who paid a royalty fee to use the Holiday Inn trademark. Holiday Inns allowed children under twelve years to stay free. From fast food to motels, family vacationing transformed the roadside landscape of America.

Ford began marketing the station wagon as a family car in 1947 but the decade of the '50s was the heyday of the station wagon.

The Ford
Station Wagon

For country estate or city home—this is the car of the year for those who demand room and smart, modern styling! Handsome, wide, roomy seats for 8. And all-around usefulness! With rear seats removed there's space to load everything—even the kitchen sink, if you like.

Carved out of solid rock on Mt. Rushmore, N. Dakota, are the faces of four great presidents. You'll recognize them — just as you recognize the rock-solid qualities of Chevrolet on your trip!

State	Number of visits
New Mexico	6,200,000
California	4,805,600
Arizona	4,200,000
Washington, D.C.	4,250,000

American Automobile Association, Americans on the Highway (1950)

ABOVE: Local Indians posed on horseback for tourists with cameras in Utah's red rock country, 1950s. Utah State Archives.

LEFT: "See the U.S.A. in your Chevrolet" was a successful sales slogan for the auto company. Chevrolet, *Holiday*, September 1951.

31

Ford's out Front with... 1

1 **"Rest-Ride" Springs!** New multi-leaf construction! You get a level, relaxed ride—even over rough roads —and new steadiness on curves!

2 **Your choice of engines!** 100 h.p. V-8 or 90 h.p. Six. Both engines with new balanced carburetion and new 4-ring aluminum pistons to save on gas and oil.

3 **Baked-enamel finish!** Ford's special enamel— baked on in a special way—is brighter and longer lasting! Because it is better bonded to the metal. That's why Ford cars *keep* their "showroom complexion."

4 **"King-size" brakes!** No other car in Ford's field has such big brakes! They're self-centering hydraulics ... give you smooth, straight stops with gentle pedal pressure.

5 **"Lifeguard" Body!** For extra safety and longer life. Ford bodies are heavy-gauge welded steel, "phosphate-coated" in Ford's special rustproofing process. Doors have double steel walls. Even the floor is steel!

There's a *Ford* in your future

Decades before safety belts would be required, car manufacturers emphasized the safety of the car's steel body and hydraulic brakes. Ford advertisement, 1946.

Chevrolet distributed this booklet to help buyers envision themselves exploring the USA in Chevrolet cars. Chevrolet Motor Division, General Motors Corporation, *See the USA Vacation and Recreation Map,* 1961.

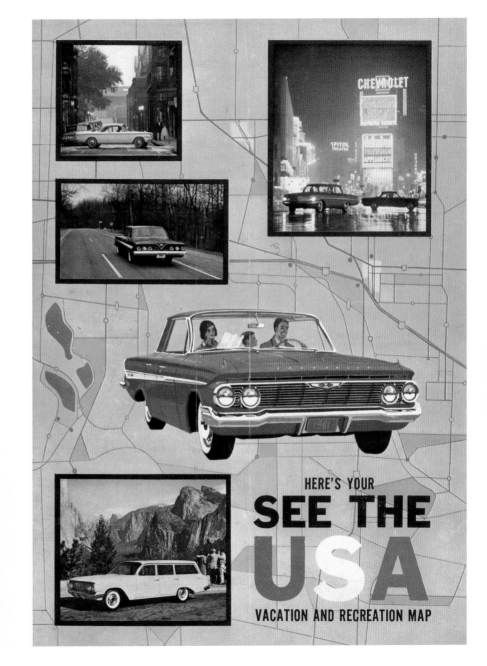

Billboard Games

"Find the alphabet. Players try to find the letters of the alphabet, in consecutive order, from billboards. They call the letters aloud as they find what they need, and should state in what word it was found. Another player may not claim that letter, but must find a different one for his score."

Frances W. Keene, Travel Fun Book for Boys and Girls *(1954)*

The backseat of the family car belonged to children. Activity books for children provided pencil games like dot-to-dot drawings of animals, matching, and crossword puzzles. Photographer Arthur Rothstein. *Look* Magazine Photograph Collection, Library of Congress.

"Vacationtime is in your heart when with a ribbon of road before you, a wonderland ahead, you deem that here, at last, is all a human can long for, till from the back seat comes a voice: 'Mom, may I have a peanut butter sandwich?'"

"The Man Next Door," Better Homes & Gardens *(August 1956)*

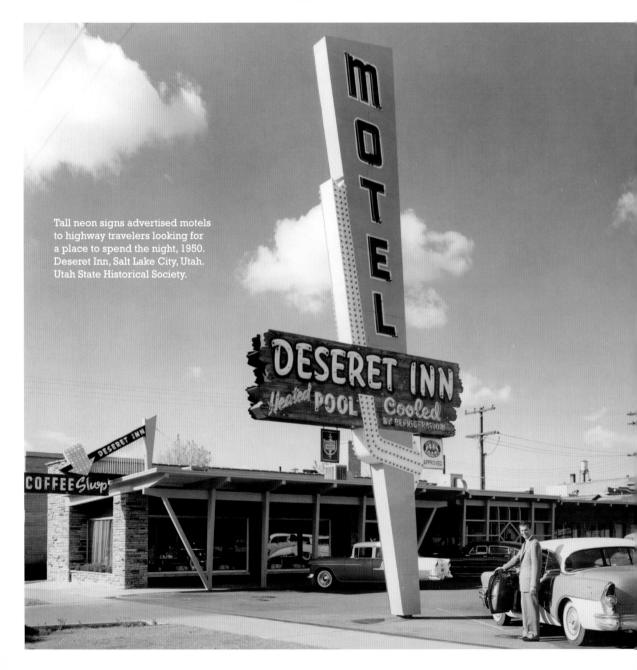

Tall neon signs advertised motels to highway travelers looking for a place to spend the night, 1950. Deseret Inn, Salt Lake City, Utah. Utah State Historical Society.

Like McDonald's, local hamburger joints sold burgers and fries at drive-in restaurants, 1961. Dee's was in Salt Lake City, Utah. Utah State Historical Society.

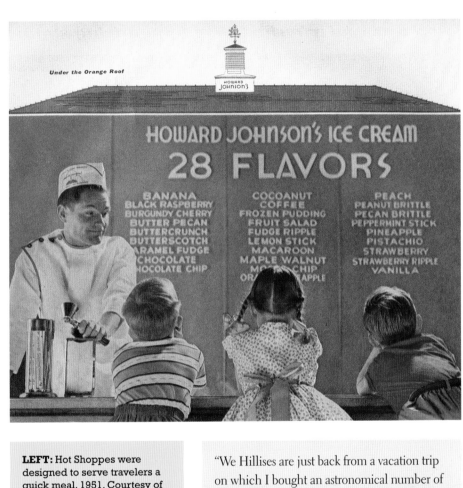

HOWARD JOHNSON'S ICE CREAM

28 FLAVORS

BANANA	COCOANUT	PEACH
BLACK RASPBERRY	COFFEE	PEANUT BRITTLE
BURGUNDY CHERRY	FROZEN PUDDING	PECAN BRITTLE
BUTTER PECAN	FRUIT SALAD	PEPPERMINT STICK
BUTTERCRUNCH	FUDGE RIPPLE	PINEAPPLE
BUTTERSCOTCH	LEMON STICK	PISTACHIO
CARAMEL FUDGE	MACAROON	STRAWBERRY
CHOCOLATE	MAPLE WALNUT	STRAWBERRY RIPPLE
CHOCOLATE CHIP	MINT CHIP	VANILLA
	ORANGE PINEAPPLE	

LEFT: Hot Shoppes were designed to serve travelers a quick meal, 1951. Courtesy of Utah State Historical Society.

ABOVE: Founded in the 1920s, Howard Johnson's chain of highway coffee shops, with their trademark orange roofs and turquoise cupolas, was among the first to welcome families with children. Advertisement, circa 1965.

"We Hillises are just back from a vacation trip on which I bought an astronomical number of hamburgers for the gastronomical delight of our children, who seem to think that American restaurants offer no other food. On the one day I insisted that we splurge with something 'different,' Mom and I ordered pheasant under glass and the kids ordered—hot dogs."

"The Man Next Door," Better Homes & Gardens *(September 1955)*

41

LEFT: Motor inns were fancier versions of motels, with more full-service features such as coffee shops. Continental Motor Lodge, 1962. Utah Postcard Collection, Marriott Library, University of Utah.

RIGHT: Advertising for Holiday Inn featured its family-friendly hospitality with a swimming pool, air-conditioning, phones in every room, and a restaurant, 1965.

LEFT: Motel postcards featured bathing beauties posing by the pool, 1960s. Se Rancho Motel, Salt Lake City, Utah. Utah Postcard Collection.

RIGHT: Motels installed water playgrounds especially for children, 1950s. Romney Motor Lodge, Salt Lake City, Utah. Utah Postcard Collection.

Families avoided the expense of bellhops by unloading the car near their room. The word "motel" was a combination of the words "motor" and "hotel," 1953. *Look* Magazine Photograph Collection, Library of Congress.

After a long day's drive, families enjoyed the refreshing water of a motel pool, 1963. *Look* Magazine Photograph Collection, Library of Congress.

CHAPTER 3

Discovering America

*H*eritage travel boomed in the decades following World War II as Americans visited the authentic sites of historic events, presidents, and patriots. War veterans toured the U.S. as an affirmation of their own values and as a means of passing them on to their children. Parents wanted their children to consider their citizenship through travel to the sacred places of America. Some American families undertook lengthy cross-country trips to see historic sites or to visit battlefields such as Gettysburg. Others took their children to colonial villages to recall the nation's founding era, or to world's fairs to celebrate the frontiers of technology in the space age. More commonly, parents took their children to Washington, D.C., to teach their children about America's heritage. In 1960, five million visits were made to the national monuments in Washington, D.C., and over eight hundred thousand people visited the White House. Traveling together as a family in a ritual of civic pilgrimage, parents and children reinforced their sense of what it meant to be American.

ABOVE: In 1953, the Whiting family of Utah drove across the country to Washington, D.C., where they made a side trip to Mount Vernon. Courtesy of Ann Whiting Orton.

LEFT: Veteran Nathan Corwin and his wife, Barbara, of suburban Philadelphia, took their three children to Washington, D.C., in 1963. They pose at the Zero Milestone near the White House.

GO FAMILY PLAN! Whether you take a weekend trip to Washington, D. C., or a vacation tour

America's schoolhouse on wheels

Our country is big and so is its history. To see even a part of it in comfort requires a full-sized American car.

Perhaps you start at a clearing in a New England woods where our forefathers had their first Thanksgiving. From there, it's a 600-mile drive to the hall where they declared their independence.

Or maybe your first stop is a courthouse in Illinois where Lincoln spoke. And from there,

your tour takes you a thousand miles across the great plains to the place where Custer stood against the Indians.

It's a big country, and our history was made all over it. The way to see it is by car. Traveling great distances is no problem in our full-sized, comfortable American cars. They're designed for the full-sized, comfortable way we like to live.

That's a Mercury Country Cruiser in the picture. It's as comfortable as it looks, with enough room to provide a home away from home for the whole family. It has the solid build that comes only with ample size. It takes you where you're

of the Old West, you can't beat the comfort, convenience and personal freedom offered by a full-sized American car.

going, smoothly and in safety. Power brakes and power steering are available to make it even easier to drive. And air conditioning can make a cool adventure out of a hot trip through the desert.

Our American cars — with all their room, comfort, and driving aids — didn't just happen. They were developed over the years to fit our American way of life. They evolved to suit the needs of a nation and a people on the move.

In a very real sense, our American cars were designed — not by the stylist, not by the engineer — but by the American people.

FORD MOTOR COMPANY THE AMERICAN ROAD, DEARBORN, MICHIGAN

The Ford Family of Fine Cars

FORD • THUNDERBIRD • EDSEL • MERCURY • LINCOLN • CONTINENTAL MARK IV

"This year why not plan your motor trips to include stops at famous historic sites along your route? There are hundreds of these cherished spots that tell the story of our country's beginnings, and its growth into a great nation. Your trips will be more exciting and educational for the youngsters, too . . . And wherever you go, tour with Texaco!"

TEXACO advertising insert in LIFE *magazine (1959)*

LEFT: In an appeal to the instincts of parents to make vacations educational, in the summer of 1959, Ford advertised its car as "America's schoolhouse on wheels." Courtesy of The Henry Ford, Dearborn, Michigan.

ABOVE: United Airlines featured a family about to board a cable car to see San Francisco's sights like Chinatown, the Harbor, and the Golden Gate Bridge. With newly affordable air travel, easterners could vacation in California without a long road or rail journey. *National Geographic,* 1950.

LEFT: Fine restaurants printed their own advertising postcards, like this one from Rice's Dining Salon on Route 66 in Amarillo, Texas. Rice's was "convenient to all highways" and approved by major dining guides and clubs. Rice's Dining Salon postcard, 1950s.

Vacation Fun...is a Family Affair
in NEW MEXICO
THE LAND OF ENCHANTMENT

Whether your vacation dreams are of action-filled days where the throbbing beat of the tom-tom heralds the beginning of an age-old Indian ceremonial dance...or whether they're of vast distances and limitless horizons hemmed in only by timbered mountain ranges towering ruggedly into turquoise skies, you'll find vacation variety in this land of romance and color! ● Here you'll discover a curious combination of the unbelievably old beside the very new...you'll savor the lingering traces of a robust Old West and an ancient Spanish culture...and you'll always remember its many sites of scenic grandeur and historical interest including eight National Monuments and Carlsbad Caverns National Park. ● Here, too, you'll discover the fascination of New Mexico, The Land of Enchantment; once you have shared it you'll never forget it!

NEW MEXICO STATE TOURIST BUREAU
Room 1350, State Capitol, Santa Fe, New Mexico
Please send free: ☐ New booklet, "Land of Enchantment," ☐ New "Recreational Map of New Mexico."

NAME...

STREET...

CITY..............................ZONE.......STATE............

Mail This Coupon
AND WE'LL SEND YOU OUR FREE MAPS AND BOOKLET PRONTO!

3-50

ABOVE: Al Uhl attempted to take a picture of his family on the steps of every state capitol in the nation. Here the family poses in front of the Nebraska state capitol, 1963. Courtesy of Lyn Uhl.

LEFT: New Mexico offered its visitors "lingering traces of a robust Old West" along with unforgettable sites of "scenic grandeur." *National Geographic,* 1950.

Visitors reverently ascend the steps to the cabin at the Abraham Lincoln Birthplace on the Lincoln Kentucky Farm on a Sunday morning in 1950. National Park Service Historic Photograph Collection, Harpers Ferry Center.

The stack of cannonballs at Shiloh National Military Park makes an interesting backdrop for a family picture, 1959. Photographer Jack E. Boucher. National Park Service Historic Photograph Collection, Harpers Ferry Center.

African American travelers discovered that to be an American was to be discriminated against. In a nation where schools, housing, and society were racially segregated, vacation lodging was also segregated by race. Segregation was legal in the South and not uncommon elsewhere in the country. It was rare to find a motel that would let blacks rent a room for the night, let alone swim in the pool. Blacks never could be sure that they would find places to sleep and eat on the road. To avoid confrontation, families commonly packed their own food and traveled at night. Many African American families ended up having to sleep in the car. The Civil Rights Act (1964) did not ensure equality, but it did make discrimination illegal and provided African Americans a tool to gain their full rights as citizens.

An African American family poses in the driveway with the family car, 1967. Photographer Bob Lerner. *Look* Magazine Photograph Collection, Library of Congress.

"For millions of Americans this is vacation time. Swarms of families load their automobiles and trek across country. I invite the members of this committee to imagine themselves darker in color and to plan an auto trip from Norfolk, Va., to the gulf coast of Mississippi, say to Biloxi. Or one from Terre Haute, Ind., to Charleston, S.C., or from Jacksonville, Fla., to Tyler, Texas. How far do you drive each day? Where and under what conditions can you and your family eat? Where can they use a restroom? Can you stop driving after a reasonable day behind the wheel or must you drive until you reach a city where relatives or friends will accommodate you and yours for the night? Will your children be denied a soft drink or an ice cream cone because they are not white?"

Roy Wilkins, NAACP, to the Committee on Commerce, United States Senate (July 22, 1963)

FACING: Dr. John O. Brown's family swims at the "only Negro motel with pool in Miami." Photographer Frank Bauman, 1959. *Look* Magazine Photograph Collection, Library of Congress.

ABOVE: In a segregated travel environment, African American travelers relied upon specialized guides to find places to stay. *The Negro Travelers' Green Book,* 1956. Schomberg Center for Research in Black Culture, New York Public Library.

The nation's beaches and municipal pools were racially segregated. Virginia Beach, Florida, was a well-known beach that was reserved for "colored only," 1959. Photographer Frank Bauman. *Look* Magazine Photograph Collection, Library of Congress.

RIGHT: *Travelguide* presented a glamorous view of travel for well-to-do African Americans. Its slogan was "Vacation and Recreation Without Humiliation." *Travelguide,* 1952. Schomberg Center for Research in Black Culture, New York Public Library.

Travelguide

1952

Price $1.00

"Vacation & Recreation Without Humiliation"

"This city, a symbol of the greatness of our republic, stirs the very fibers of his heart as he reflects that it stands for 'one nation, indivisible, with Liberty and Justice for All.' No matter how lowly or humble he may be, when he experiences the majesty of the Capitol, or the strong simplicity of the White House, he will realize that Washington is, in part his, and he will feel as did George Washington, Thomas Jefferson, Abraham Lincoln with millions of other Americans, the strength and enduring permanence of those ideals of democracy forming the foundation of this city and this nation. He and generations of Americans to come will gain inspiration from this city to make those ideals a part of their lives and our nation's living history."

Lewis J. Nesterman, Washington Handy Guide (1942)

© B.S.REYNOLDS CO.

The Lincoln Memorial was a must-see monument on any tourist's Washington, D.C., itinerary. Postcards presented a more stately view than could be achieved by an amateur with a travel camera. B. S. Reynolds postcard, 1940s.

RIGHT: The Corwins gaze upward to the capitol rotunda during their 1963 visit. Courtesy of Andrea L. Weitzman.

Union Station, Washington, D. C.

C-8   (C) Underwood & Underwood

Hotel Statler

WASHINGTON
D. C.

FACING ABOVE: Watercolor scenes printed on linen paper were popular postcards for tourists long after modern color printing techniques were invented. Union Station, Washington, D.C., was the entry point for many tourists to the nation's capital. Underwood & Underwood postcard, 1940s.

FACING BELOW: Hotel Statler's postcards featured a montage of local landmarks, emphasizing the hotel's central place in the nation's capital. Hotel Statler postcard, 1950s.

RIGHT: Map covers featured families exploring the landmarks of the nation's capital city. Esso, General Drafting Co., *Washington D.C. and Vicinity Map and Visitor's Guide,* 1957.

Washington, D.C. and vicinity

MAP AND VISITOR'S GUIDE

ESSO

Smithsonian Institution
(SEE COVER STORY INSIDE)

White House, Washington, D. C.

ABOVE: This vintage linen postcard features the north portico and reflecting pool of the White House, home of the U.S. President and his family and always a popular visitor spot on a tour of Washington. Foster & Reynolds.

FACING: Parks photographers promoted family travel by picturing children, such as this boy and girl with a cannon at Antietam National Battlefield, 1961. Photographer Jack E. Boucher. National Park Service Historic Photograph Collection, Harpers Ferry Center.

"Every American, from childhood on, is imaginatively and emotionally attracted to see his nation's capital. He knows he will feel at home, even before he gets there—for this wondrous, shining city belongs to all Americans."

D.C. Transit System, Sightseeing in Washington D.C. & Vicinity *(1964)*

New England has _everything_ you "go" for!

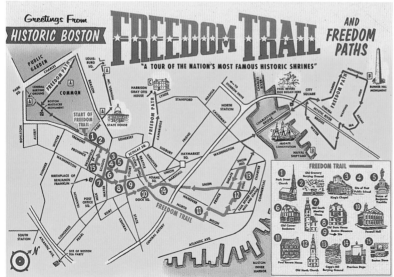

Greetings From **HISTORIC BOSTON**

FREEDOM TRAIL AND FREEDOM PATHS

"A TOUR OF THE NATION'S MOST FAMOUS HISTORIC SHRINES"

ABOVE: Many families would travel to New England, touring the historic sites and enjoying the beautiful scenery of the East. *National Geographic,* 1954.

LEFT: To bring more tourists to Boston, the Freedom Trail was marked in 1951 to guide visitors to the important "historic shrines." This postcard features the red line added in the 1960s to make it easier for tourists to navigate their way to sites like the Old North Church.

FACING: Jeanne Allred poses in the stocks on the green in a colonial village in Massachusetts, 1958. Courtesy of Susan Whetstone.

The Lure of the Wild West

Children's enthusiasm for television westerns helped make the West a prime vacation destination in the postwar era. Children idolized their television western heroes such as Annie Oakley, Hopalong Cassidy, Roy Rogers, and the Lone Ranger, and they wanted a chance to live out their fantasies in the West. During a time when the population of the country was moving west for opportunity, children's parents also hungered to see the West of the westerns.

Many Americans sought the adventure of the Old West by staying at dude ranches. Dude ranches sold an authentic western experience like the scenes vacationers saw in television Westerns, complete with horseback and stagecoach rides. With their hearty cooking and rustic yet modern cabins, dude ranches offered the comforts of the new West with the attractions of the Old West.

By visiting the West's ghost towns and modern cities, families could combine the Old West with the new West on their road trips. Families from

ABOVE: Going to Knott's Berry Farm gave every child a chance to be an Indian, 1970s. Courtesy of Tiffany Taylor.

LEFT: Chevrolet cars boasted ample "horsepower" to traverse the most rugged roads in the West. Magazine advertisement, 1953.

colder climates basked in the sunny Southern California weather as they drove to the beach or ate a picnic lunch under the palms.

The cowboy craze and the selling of the West as a vacation destination made western-themed amusement parks in Southern California popular destinations for families on vacation. Instead of visiting a dude ranch, it was less expensive to visit Southern California's amusement parks with their staged recreations of the Old West.

The Knott's Berry Farm theme park originated as a berry stand during the Great Depression when Mother (Cordelia) Knott began serving chicken dinners to boost profits. In 1940, Walter Knott bought the ghost town of Calico in the Mojave Desert and carted back its buildings to create a replica of a mining town in Buena Park. By 1953, Knott's Berry Farm covered forty acres and provided enough parking for four thousand cars. That year there were more than 1.2 million visitors. Children enjoyed panning for gold in a millrace while being watched over by a grizzly prospector or posing with Indians in feathered headdresses. Visitors were fond of posing for snapshots with the statues of the gold miners or saloon girls in Ghost Town, creating a memory of their visit to the Old West at Knott's Berry Farm.

The West's second major amusement park, Disneyland, opened on July 17, 1955, to instant success. Within a month, over twenty thousand people were visiting each day, accounting for about half of the tourists to Southern California. Frontierland featured the adventure of the Wild West for children and their families, allowing them to board a stagecoach or ride in a Conestoga wagon. Visitors traveled aboard a stern-wheeler like the ones that plied the Mississippi to Tom Sawyer's Island or toured a Western mining town. On the Mule Pack ride, a trail boss led each train of seven to eight mules, with smaller mules and child riders at the front. Children danced the Friendship Dance with "real" Indians at the "authentic Indian Village" in Frontierland.

As the western craze faded in the sixties, Disneyland offered modern versions of the West that attracted family tourists. Families viewed the future at Tomorrowland, where futuristic rides like the submarine cruise opened in 1959. The Trip to the Moon ride delivered "the sights, sounds and sensations of the half-million mile journey" to the moon that was still a dream for the future. By 1966, Disneyland featured nearly fifty major attractions and had drawn almost fifty million visitors.

Saddle up the station wagon! Like the settlers in their covered wagons, modern Americans conquered the West in their cars. Families loaded their station wagons and drove west for adventure in postwar America. Magazine advertisement, 1953.

IT'S *Colorado* CALLING

"As soon as summer arrives—and with rail travel conditions greatly improved —we'll be looking for you."

Yes, it's Colorado calling . . . the Colorado of mighty mountains and singing streams . . . invigorating sun-warmed days and restful blanket nights.

When you go, there's the swift Union Pacific Streamliner "City of Denver"—overnight, everynight, between Chicago and Denver; also fine train service from other points east and west of Denver. Your journey by rail will be the high spot of your vacation or business trip.

Remember that Union Pacific also serves California, the Pacific Northwest, and a number of famous National Parks such as Yellowstone; more western scenic regions, in fact, than any other railroad. It's the world's greatest vacation travel bargain.

For unexcelled rail service, to or from the West, go Union Pacific.

be Specific—say "Union Pacific"

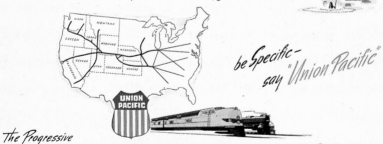

The Progressive
UNION PACIFIC RAILROAD
ROAD OF THE *Streamliners* AND THE *Challengers*

"We aim to keep you comfortable and give you home-cooked meals while you enjoy these WESTERN EXPERIENCES."

"For a Real Vacation Come to a Colorado Dude Ranch This Year" (1953)

The Byron Wingett family ride horseback at a Montana dude ranch, 1963. Photographers Bob Sandberg and Ben Kocivar. *Look* Magazine Photograph Collection, Library of Congress.

FACING: Railroads urged travelers to "go Union Pacific" to western states like Colorado with its "mighty mountains and singing streams . . . invigorating sun-warmed days and restful blanket nights." *National Geographic,* 1946.

ABOVE: The "wandering Wingetts" ride in a replica of a western stagecoach, 1963. Photographers Bob Sandberg and Ben Kocivar. *Look* Magazine Photograph Collection, Library of Congress.

FACING: The Wingetts find respite in a mountain cabin, 1963. Photographers Bob Sandberg and Ben Kocivar. *Look* Magazine Photograph Collection, Library of Congress.

THIS FALL *join the fun in Southern California!*

In Fall, our "second Summer," celebrations, rodeos and all kinds of festivities seem to start by spontaneous combustion throughout Southern California. It's a time when you can enjoy everything you've heard about here—a vacation time when gay, exciting things are going on.

So plan to join the fun in Los Angeles County and all Southern California *this Fall*. Coupon will bring you full information.

1 FOREIGN QUARTERS ARE FUN . . . the Mexican market place with its Spanish dancers, pottery makers, glass blowers . . . and Chinatowns with their stone dragons, miniature gardens, restaurants, curio stores, and quaint shopkeepers.

2 BEACH PARTIES ARE IN ORDER . . . to the music of Pacific combers on beaches especially designed for sunlazing. In Fall, days are warm and sun-flooded—the water inviting.

3 SWIM IN THE DESERT . . . It's no mirage, that water; just one of many luxurious pools at desert resorts. Get a sun tan while you play your favorite sport or ride the desert trails.

4 NIGHT LIFE IN FULL SWING . . . Screen and radio stars swarm to smart night clubs where you, too, can dine, dance, watch a glittering floor show, hear famous name bands.

ALL-YEAR CLUB OF SOUTHERN CALIFORNIA, LTD.

This advertisement sponsored by the Los Angeles County Board of Supervisors for the citizens of Beverly Hills, Glendale, Hollywood, Long Beach, Los Angeles, Pasadena, Pomona, Santa Monica and 182 other communities. Copyright, 1947, by All-Year Club of Southern California, Ltd. —a non-profit community organization serving vacationists.

FREE FOLDER—MAIL COUPON TODAY

5 GALA AND SPECTACULAR SPORTS EVENTS . . . Join the summery crowds at big, exciting football games . . . golf tournaments . . . tennis matches . . . rodeos . . . speedboat contests.

6 "WARNING—DEER ON HIGHWAY" . . . A common mountain scene. Thrill to challenging peaks, jeweled lakes, fragrant forests, alpine blossoms . . . all from superb highways.

> All-Year Club of So. Calif., Dept. C-6
> 629 S. Hill St., Los Angeles 14, Calif.
> Please send me your free vacation folder "WHAT TO DO AND SEE IN SOUTHERN CALIFORNIA."
>
> Name_____
> Street_____
> City_____ Zone____
> State_____
> — (PLEASE PRINT NAME AND ADDRESS) —

WHEN YOU ARRIVE IN LOS ANGELES, VISIT OUR ALL-YEAR CLUB VISITORS' BUREAU, 517 WEST 6TH ST., FOR FREE, FRIENDLY VACATION SERVICE AND COMPLETE INFORMATION.

The Herricks enjoy an outdoor picnic under the palms in Southern California, 1953. Photographer Rupert Allen. *Look* Magazine Photograph Collection, Library of Congress.

The Herricks spend a day at Knott's Berry Farm in Buena Park, California, 1953. Part of the attraction was the Ghost Town and Calico Railroad, which made six trips a day and was regularly held up by outlaws to the delight of the visitors. Photographer Rupert Allen. *Look* Magazine Photograph Collection, Library of Congress.

The Herrick children pan for gold under the watchful eye of an old forty-niner, 1953. Photographer Rupert Allen. *Look* Magazine Photograph Collection, Library of Congress.

FACING: The Herrick boys pose with Indians in ceremonial dress at Knott's Berry Farm, 1953. Photographer Rupert Allen. *Look* Magazine Photograph Collection, Library of Congress.

ABOVE: The Herricks pose for a picture with Handsome Brady and Whiskey Bill in Ghost Town, 1953. Photographer Rupert Allen. *Look* Magazine Photograph Collection, Library of Congress.

THIS SUMMER AND FALL...
VACATIONS AGAIN IN
Southern California

YES, during the coming summer-fall season, Southern California will start welcoming vacationers again. As the flow of returning Pacific veterans tapers off, our hotels will have more and more rooms available for visitors. Of course, *it will be essential to have confirmed accommodations in advance*...and the later you can come, the easier it will be to get reservations.

In Southern California, summer continues to November...bright, warm days...cool nights...little or no rain. Send for a FREE COLOR FOLDER that's packed with information about this year-round vacation land. Mail the coupon today!

Bring a camera for beach shots: sun-lazing on clean, white sand, riding a surfboard, sailing to pleasure isles...close-ups in Chinatown, the unique Mexican quarter, the old Spanish missions...action shots at the races, tennis and polo matches, or on palm-bordered fairways.

Prepare for contrasts: lush orange groves beneath high mountain peaks...tropic fruits — date palms, cherimoyas — but a few miles from alpine flowers beside glacial lakes...ancient fossil pits near ultra-modern shops...latest jet planes flying over historic Spanish ranchos.

Bring a light coat for cool nights. Thrill to symphonies, movie previews, premieres, hilltop views of millions of lights in sixty cities far below, gay night spots where top-flight bands, spectacular floor shows entertain movie stars and *you*.

Get set for magnificent views...for boating on mile-high lakes...ride, climb, relax. Sleep soundly under blankets. Adventure, variety, sun, rest—these make a vacation in Los Angeles County and all Southern California an unforgettable experience.

ABOVE: This postwar pitch to American families touted the beaches, lush gardens, and glamour of Southern California. "Adventure, variety, sun, and rest" appealed to a nation recovering from wartime. *National Geographic,* 1947.

RIGHT: The favorite family photo spot in Disneyland was in front of Sleeping Beauty's Castle. The Trevor family visit Disneyland with their grandparents, 1956. Shades of L.A. Collection, Los Angeles Public Library.

Family vacationers wrote home to relatives on postcards like these from the 1950s and 1960s, saying that Disneyland was a "fantastic place." Author's collection.

Children take part in the Friendship Dance at Indian Village in Frontierland at Disneyland, 1958. Courtesy of Barbara Robeson.

Disneyland Facts

22
Attractions in 1955

47
Attractions in 1965

$0.50
Visitor fee for children in 1955

$3.00
Visitor fee for children in 1965

150
Average number of babies visiting the Baby Station per day in 1962

250
Lost children each week in summer 1962

20,000
Daily visitors after Disneyland opened on July 17, 1955

467,730
Hot dogs sold in the first 6 months after opening

558,324
Ice cream bars sold in the first 6 months after opening

10,000,000
Davy Crockett coonskin caps sold in 1955–56

"Vacationland" Disney News, *various years*

ABOVE: Little girls in matching dresses pose with the whale in Fantasyland, 1956. Courtesy of Sterling D. Sessions.

RIGHT: At Disneyland, children could relive the fantasies of Walt Disney's movies, like *Snow White and the Seven Dwarfs.*

Foods Eaten at Disneyland in 1970

87,000	Hot dogs, pounds		**500,000**	Hamburger meat, pounds
98,000	Jell-O, pounds		**1,000,000**	Ice cream cones
100,000	Ice cream, gallons		**2,500,000**	Ice cream bars
174,000	Popcorn, pounds			

Disney News, *spring 1970*

Disneyland offered a glimpse of the future on the Submarine Voyage and the Kaiser Aluminum Telescope in Tomorrowland.

The Great Outdoors

Camping became a common family vacation choice in postwar America because it was an inexpensive, fun, and wholesome way to be outdoors. The groundswell of enthusiasm for camping surged throughout the decade; camper registration totaled ten million in 1950 and tripled to thirty million by 1960. Parents took their children camping to acquaint them with nature. Children were thought to be natural campers, curious explorers who needed to take only a few precautions for their own safety. Camping was seen as a way to teach children responsibility for themselves and others in a safe environment. While most families camped out of their cars, the invention of portable camper shells mounted on the back of pickup trucks, and the manufacture of RVs (recreational vehicles) offered even more features of home on the road.

The national parks were a favorite location for families to camp. The total number of visits to national parks rose from 21.7 million in 1946 to 61.6 million in 1956, the year Mission 66 was announced. Under Mission 66, an ambitious program to upgrade park facilities to meet the needs of

ABOVE: Maps feature mountain scenes. Sinclair, *Western United States,* circa 1950s.

LEFT: The use of passenger vans allowed families to take along more equipment and camp more comfortably. Chevrolet Motor Division, General Motors Corporation, *See the USA Vacation and Travel Map,* 1961.

tourists, the government spent over $1 billion to build parking lots, roads, new campgrounds, and picnic areas. By the time Mission 66 was complete ten years later, visitation was over 133 million. The national parks with parking lots, cafeterias, lodges, and trailer parks, were hardly wilderness. But it was as close as many families in America could get to nature, and it was nature at a price they could afford.

Parks offered activities for every member of the family: hiking, nature walks with rangers, fishing, horseback riding, or driving along the scenic park roads. The parks established programs and museums to educate the tourists who wanted to learn about the natural environment. Thousands of tourists attended the campfire programs with slides where they were taught about park history, plants, geology, and wildlife. Still, the parks could be dangerous for children due to the hazards of boiling thermal pools, steep canyons, swift-moving rivers, and hungry bears.

"Camping, today, is for everyone. Your family can pack up for a weekend—or a month—in state and national parks across the land. It's an inexpensive, carefree way to have fun together."

"The How-to of Family Camping,"
Better Homes & Gardens *(May 1958)*

Camper's Checklist

Standard: tent, stove, bedding, silverware, plates, cups, etc.
Cooking utensils: frying pan, stew pots, coffee pot, can opener, knives, bottle opener, spatula, cooking forks, roasting forks, serving spoons.
Camp living necessities: soap, detergent, paper napkins, wax paper, toilet paper, paper towels, pot cleaners, pot holders, gallon thermos jug, rain coats or umbrella, warm jackets and caps, extra pair of shoes, mosquito repellent and medication, toilet and shaving articles, toothbrushes and paste, dishcloths and towels, washcloths and bath towels, plastic tablecloth.

Rand McNally Campground Guide:
A Family Camping Directory *(1963)*

Annual Visits to National Parks

Year	Number of Visits
1945	**11,715,797**
1950	**33,254,539**
1960	**79,230,960**
1965	**121,313,965**
1970	**172,006,570**
1975	**190,392,575**

National Park Service Public Use Statistics Office

Camping requires a variety of
equipment, and this cartoon makes
fun of the task of unloading the
family car with stoves, tents, and
gear. *Field and Stream,* 1960.

"America's national parks and monuments offer the country's most flexible vacations among the greatest spectacles of nature . . . Free to all, preserved for all, these 20,000,000 acres are the past's living heritage, a bridge from all time to our time. They are a magic haven from the traffic and tension of everyday routine."

"Your America," Ladies Home Journal *(June 1947)*

ABOVE: Homemade car-top carriers allowed a family to carry all its gear to the national parks, 1965. Courtesy of Christopher Johnson.

FACING: Travel trailers were a home away from home while camping. Acadia National Park, 1958. Photographer Richard G. Smithe. Courtesy of National Park Service Historic Photograph Collection, Harpers Ferry Center.

Try These Recipes for Better Outdoor Eating!

Fricasseed Chicken and Dumplings, Roast Duck, Swiss Steak, Boiled Fish with Butter Dressing, Fish Cakes, New England Clam Chowder, Hard-Shelled Crabs, Sourdough Rolls, Picnic Burgers Deluxe, Dogs-in-a Blanket, and Kabobs.

More Fun Outdoors with Coleman *(1953)*

ABOVE: Camping with children involved taking along substantial amounts of food and equipment, including a table cloth. Buffalo Forest Camp, Targhee National Forest, Idaho, 1958. Photograph by Bluford W. Muir. Courtesy of USDA Forest Service.

BELOW: Lightweight tents and camping equipment made of nylon and aluminum components became more widely available in the 1960s. Photographers Bob Sandberg and Ben Kocivar. *Look* Magazine Photograph Collection, Library of Congress.

Dog-in-a-Blanket

"To achieve a delicious variation on the usual frankfurter, wrap a strip of bacon spirally around each frank, fastening each end with a half toothpick. Grill until the bacon is crisp all around, remove the toothpick halves and serve in buns."

More Fun Outdoors with Coleman (1953)

S'mores

"Make a sandwich out of a piece of chocolate and two graham crackers. Toast marshmallow to a golden brown. Put into the sandwich between the chocolate and the cracker; press gently together, and eat."

Cooking Out-of-Doors (1946)

Roasting marshmallows made camping fun for children, 1960s. Courtesy of Lucy Moore Brown.

ABOVE: A park ranger shows a young rider how to handle a horse at Skyland stables in Shenandoah National Park, 1958. Photograph by Jack E. Boucher. Courtesy of National Park Service Historic Photograph Collection, Harpers Ferry Center.

FACING ABOVE: The park naturalist leads a group of visitors on a nature walk in Shenandoah National Park, 1950. Photograph by Arthur F. Fawcett. Courtesy of National Park Service Historic Photograph Collection, Harpers Ferry Center.

FACING BELOW: A father and his daughter pose with their cameras by the trailhead sign before hiking in Great Smoky Mountains National Park, 1950s. Private collection.

"There's a revolution in recreation underway in America. More leisure time, higher incomes, better transportation and renewed emphasis on family 'togetherness' have put the focus of family fun on the great outdoors. Families are discovering the wide open spaces on their vacations—spending their weekends fishing the lakes, the streams, hunting the rugged backwoods country, hiking the mountain trails, camping in the quiet solitude of our magnificent national and state parks."

More Fun Outdoors with Coleman (1953)

LEFT: The educational features of the parks were popular with parents who sent their children on nature hikes with the rangers. The Junior Nature study group listens to a park ranger explain about the eating habits of moose in Yellowstone in 1948. National Park Service, Photograph Collection.

ABOVE: Children gather as a Yosemite National Park ranger shows them how to make a monkey flower move, 1970. Courtesy of National Park Service Historic Photograph Collection, Harpers Ferry Center.

At Yellowstone, driving through the park could be dangerous
because bears begged for food from passing cars, 1958.
Photographer Jack E. Boucher. Courtesy of National Park Service
Historic Photograph Collection, Harpers Ferry Center.

LEFT: Bears at Yellowstone would often visit family campsites and
dumpsters, helping themselves to any food they could get their
paws on. *Holiday,* 1951.

Parks could be dangerous places for children playing along the Firehole River in Upper Geyser Basin, Yellowstone National Park, 1955. National Park Service Photograph Collection.

"Yellowstone, of all the national parks, is the wildest and most universal in its appeal . . . Daily new, always strange, ever full of change, it is Nature's wonder park. It is the most human and the most popular of all the parks."

Yellowstone Park for Your Vacation (*circa 1920s*)

TOURAIDE
map of
**YELLOWSTONE
NATIONAL PARK**

78

CONOCO

ABOVE: Oil companies promoted travel by supplying specialized maps. Map of Yellowstone National Park. Continental Oil Company, Conoco, 1977.

RIGHT: Crowds gather to see the eruption of Old Faithful at Yellowstone, 1963. Photographers Bob Sandberg and Ben Kocivar. *Look* Magazine Photograph Collection, Library of Congress.

Queen's Garden

TRAIL LEAFLET

Bryce Canyon National Park

Queen's Garden

10¢

ABOVE: Children sit atop a stone wall at a scenic overlook in the Grand Tetons, Wyoming, 1962. Courtesy of Marybeth Lathen.

FACING ABOVE: Family photographers often posed their subjects on the edge of a precipice or at a designated overlook to achieve a scenic family portrait. A father and son overlook Zion Canyon, 1957. Courtesy of Craig Harline.

FACING BELOW: The Rugh children of Los Angeles pose at the edge of the Grand Canyon on their last family trip together, 1969. Courtesy of Barbara R. Robeson.

FACING FAR LEFT: Trail guides helped tourists find their way on hikes through the parks. *Queen's Garden Trail Leaflet*, Bryce Canyon National Park, 1960s. Courtesy of Barbara R. Robeson.

"Today, Americans are crowding the highways and visiting the parks as never before in history. Yearly visits to the national parks have leaped from 22 million only 15 years ago to more than 80 million last year.

"The National Park system affords Americans opportunities to enjoy great scenic and inspirational areas of their country in a natural, unspoiled condition and the rare quality of the primitive wilderness that was America before it was touched by civilization. They may better comprehend the physical and spiritual links that bind America's past to its present and future and they may find release from the care and tension of the workaday world."

National Park Service Annual Report *(1962)*

CHAPTER 6

Sand, Sun, and Fun in the Water

Families who lived close to the water drove to the nation's lakes, rivers, and beaches to cool off in the hot summer. In the Midwest, vacationers drove north to fish, swim, and boat in the many lakes surrounded by tall pines. Summer resorts in the country provided a welcoming vacation place for families who returned each year. Family-owned resorts gave vacationers a chance to spend their days outdoors swimming, fishing, or horseback riding. Resorts ranged from rustic cabins to large lodges where guests could mingle and participate in planned activities. The invention of affordable powerboats and the creation of reservoirs in the West beckoned summer vacationers to swim, fish, and water-ski in the cool water.

On the coast, beaches were attractive destinations for families who enjoyed cooling off in the ocean waves, building sandcastles, and picnicking while soaking up the sun. Florida and California built their vacation business by publicizing their beaches as the perfect place for a fun day in the sun.

ABOVE: Beach scene on map. Sinclair, *Western United States,* circa 1950s.

LEFT: The Daytona Beach Resort Area in Florida promoted its beaches by distributing images like the one of this family that posed for the photographer, 1960s. The Henry Ford.

113

THINGS LOOK BRIGHT ALL OVER WITH THAT

GOLDEN
Florida
GLOW!

A fabulous state of well-being...
which makes everything
seem bright and shining
...and *extra special!*

ABOVE LEFT: Mom, dad, and the kids could get that Golden Florida Glow traveling on a magic carpet to an "extra special" place "at rates to make your vacation budget smile." *National Geographic,* 1954.

ABOVE RIGHT : A traveling family stops to picnic on the Sunshine Skyway at St. Petersburg, Florida, 1957. The Henry Ford.

"Sun time is fun time—family style—at the Daytona Beach Resort
Area. Relaxin', restin', and recreation are just three of the many
things to do at the World's Most Famous Beach."

Daytona Beach brochure (1958)

ABOVE: Florida offered other attractions besides its beaches. A curving palm tree framed this promotional photograph for Silver Springs, 1955. Photographer Bruce Mozert. The Henry Ford.

FACING: Tourists in Key West, Florida, ride the Conch Tour Train, 1962. The Henry Ford.

"Regardless of where boating enthusiasts live, there are usually rivers, lakes or coastal water within driving distance where they can enjoy their hobby . . . Many family men justify their investment in one of the new type cruisers on the score that it allows them to enjoy a hobby they have always dreamed about—and yet be able to spend more time with the family."

"The Big Revolution in Boating," Better Homes & Gardens *(August 1955)*

TAN...don't burn...use COPPERTONE

Get a faster, _deeper_ tan plus GUARANTEED sunburn protection!

Sunbalanced Screening does it! With Coppertone, you get a faster, smoother, *deeper* tan, with maximum sunburn protection—than with any other leading product! That's because Coppertone's special screening agent, homomenthyl salicylate, lets *in* the ultraviolet tanning rays that activate coloring matter deep within your skin...as it shuts *out* rays that burn and coarsen your skin.

Conditions Skin, too! The extra lanolin and other protectives in Coppertone keep it on the skin longer, protect you even after swimming. Coppertone prevents ugly drying and peeling, too.

America's Favorite! Originated in sunny Florida, Coppertone now far outsells all other suntan products. Use it whenever you're out in the sun—at beach, pool, fishing, or right in your own backyard. Available in Lotion, Oil, Cream, Spray, and new Coppertone Shade for children and those with sensitive skin. Also Noskote. Get a rich, long-lasting Coppertone tan! Get Coppertone in large size to save most.

COPPERTONE
Suntan Lotion

Also available in Canada
Another quality product
of Plough, Inc.

Don't be a paleface!

LEFT: Coppertone Suntan Lotion made its product famous with this unforgettable image of a little girl at the beach. *Ladies Home Journal,* 1959.

ABOVE: Shallow waters of the Great Salt Lake make a perfect wading pool for Kay Harline and her son. 1968. Courtesy of Craig Harline.

FACING: Even children could catch big fish at Gilman's resort on Mitchell Lake in Minnesota, 1950s. Minnesota Historical Society.

At Gilman's resort in northern Minnesota, children enjoy fishing and boating under the watchful eye of their parents, 1950s. Minnesota Historical Society.

ABOVE: Lake cabins were usually primitive with few amenities, but the setting near the lake brought the family back to nature. Cabin No. 7 at Gilman's resort, 1940s. Minnesota Historical Society.

"If you've got a king-size family and a taste for fun to match—this is for you! Load up with all the gear that goes with a weekend of wonderful living."

Evinrude advertisement (1959)

LEFT: Romances bloomed during summers in the countryside. Lake Geneva, Wisconsin, 1930s. Courtesy of Caye Wycoff.

RIGHT: New technologies made powerboats affordable and lightweight, like this Johnson Sea-Horse V-75 that had "muscle enough to make even a family-loaded cruiser feel as frisky as a runabout." *Field and Stream*, March 1960.

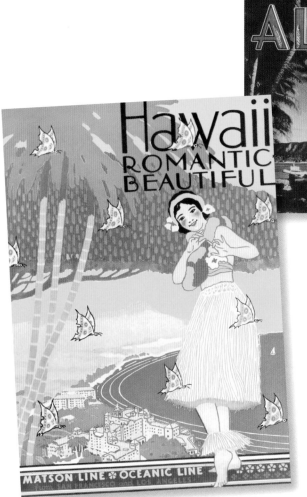

ABOVE: A postcard souvenir features an outrigger and a surfer at Waikiki Beach, 1951.

LEFT: Free postcards and booklets conveyed the idea that Hawaii was "romantic" and "beautiful." Matson Line and Oceanic Line Tourist booklet, 1940s.

RIGHT: United Airlines offered a low price of $270 for a round trip from California to Hawaii in only hours, making the exotic more available to American travelers who viewed this colorful advertisement. *National Geographic,* 1950.

BELOW: A line of hula dancers suggests the exotic possibilities of a vacation in Hawaii, 1951.

See beautiful Hawaii in "Million Dollar Weekend," an Eagle-Lion release starring Gene Raymond, Stephanie Paull and Francis Lederer.

Hawaii—
Only hours away by United!

BE THERE FOR COLORFUL ALOHA WEEK, NOV. 14 THROUGH 21

With United Air Lines' all DC-6 Mainliner 300 service, you can leave New York at midnight and be in Hawaii at 6:10 p.m.—*in time for dinner!* Yes, it's only a few hours to these isles of enchantment—and the magic begins when you board your luxurious DC-6 Mainliner 300. United's service is the fastest by hours, and the finest over the Pacific. You enjoy stroll-about spaciousness of the huge, pressurized cabin. Superb full-course steak dinner. Gay holiday informality of a taste-tempting buffet. Added service features you'll find on no other airliner in the world. And the cost—so low it will amaze you. You can go or return by way of Los Angeles and San Francisco at no extra cost.

Only $270 Round Trip
from San Francisco or Los Angeles
plus 15% Federal Tax
MAKE YOUR RESERVATIONS NOW THROUGH YOUR TRAVEL AGENT

THE MAIN LINE AIRWAY
PASSENGERS • MAIL • EXPRESS

UNITED AIR LINES

You've always wanted to come ...why not **THIS FALL!**

● You'll wear a flower lei to a luau... intriguing South Sea feast. You'll see true island hulas danced under a tropical moon. You'll watch the people who first carved out surfboards ride them off Waikiki. Gardens bright with tropic flowers...golf on palm-bordered fairways green the year round...the dramatic interest of Pearl Harbor...all that colorful dream you've had of Hawaii will become a reality.

Hawaii

No passport, no foreign exchange to bother with. Enjoying American standards of living, you'll roam among tropic isles excitingly different and new! ● Air and steamship lines link Hawaii with San Francisco, Los Angeles, Portland, Seattle, Vancouver. You can go one way by air, the other by sea or round trip by either. ● From Honolulu, island of Oahu, you can fly in about an hour or less to any of the other major Hawaiian islands—Maui, Hawaii, Kauai. Let your Travel Agent help you plan to include them. You can see them all at moderate cost.

Hawaii will delight you any month in the year!

ALOHA WEEK — **Oct. 22 to 29**
... Hawaii's unique, picturesque carnival of ancient South Sea sports, music, dancing and pageantry...will be the climax of your fall vacation!

HAWAII VISITORS BUREAU

A non-profit organization maintained for your service by

THE PEOPLE OF HAWAII

A 4½ DAY CRUISE BY LUXURY LINER

8½ HOURS BY LUXURY PLANE

When sunning—remember that the sun is strong "medicine" and that sunburn causes an annual loss of several million work days. So, take the sun in small doses—about 10 minutes the first day, 20 the second. Sunburn usually can be prevented by applying a "sun-protective" preparation to the skin before exposure. However, to protect yourself against sunstroke or heatstroke, always avoid long, direct exposure to the sun.

Transportation companies distributed color postcards and brochures as advertising souvenirs for travel to Hawaii. United Airlines travel poster, 1940s.

Vacationers were cautioned by Metropolitan Life to "Always avoid long, direct exposure to the sun" and to use protective sun lotion. *National Geographic*, 1951.

Epilogue

The family vacation is being reinvented, but it is inspired by memories of vacations of the past. Vacations are still seen as an escape, a way to bring the family together, and a chance for parents to spend more time with their children. The older baby boomers are going gray, but they have not given up the family vacation. They take their children and grandchildren on cruises or buy RVs and drive around the country sightseeing and visiting. As they take their offspring on vacation, they will continue to remember the family vacations of their own childhood.